The Miracles of Jesus

Written by
Dee Leone

Illustrated by
Jeff Van Kanegan

Cover Illustrated by
Judy Hierstein

Cover Designed by
Nehmen-Kodner

A Division of Frank Schaffer Publications, Inc.
23740 Hawthorne Blvd., Torrance, CA 90505

Dedication

This book of miracles is dedicated to my little daughter, Rachelle, a wonderful miracle of God's love.

Table of Contents

Introduction

Young children will have a wonderful time as they learn about the fascinating and incredible work Jesus did here on earth. This book contains delightful picture stories of Jesus' miracles, activity pages to reinforce each story, and songs and ideas to supplement each of the seven units. The pages of each unit can be put together to form keepsake booklets about each miracle.

Each unit begins with a simplified Bible story given in words and pictures. Children can participate in the reading of each story by supplying the word for each given picture (see pages 4–5 for descriptions) while the parent or teacher reads the text. Children can then use the picture clues to retell the story in their own words. Finally, the children can color the pictures.

In addition to the picture stories are exciting and stimulating activity pages to go along with each story. (An answer key is provided on page 48.) They reinforce story concepts and provide practice with numbers, colors, opposites, making comparisons, and other skills. Very young children who have not yet developed small motor skills will enjoy doing many of the activities orally. Older children will be able to complete the written activities after an adult or older child reads the directions to them. It is suggested that one part of the directions at a time be read. As a child completes the activity which corresponds to a specific part of the directions, additional directions can be read.

Bible verses on the activity pages are provided as a reference. They are taken from the New International Version of the Bible. They can be read to the children or used to help explain to the children what the activities are about. Older children can memorize some of the simpler parts of the verses.

Each unit ends with an idea page filled with songs, projects, discussion topics, and more, dedicated to enriching the Bible story. This idea page can be used in the classroom or sent home.

Located on pages 4 and 5 are stickers relating to each story. Review these so that you can let the children know what or whom each picture represents. Then make copies of these for the children. The stickers can be cut out by children who have developed adequate motor skills, or an adult or older child can cut out the stickers for very young children. After reviewing the names of the sticker shapes (circle, square, rectangle, etc.), let the children color them with markers or crayons. They can then be used for a wonderful variety of activities and crafts. For example, a mixture of water and glue or mucilage can be added to the backs, and the stickers can be used for decorating stationery, for sealing envelopes, as rewards, etc. Or, they can be strung together to make Bible story necklaces or placed on small banners. Or, enlarge them for use on greeting cards, bulletin board displays, or mobiles. They can also be enlarged, mounted on heavy paper, and cut into pieces to make puzzles.

All of the pages and ideas in this book provide a wonderful way to introduce children to the cherished stories of the miracles Jesus performed. You will love watching the children have fun as they learn valuable skills and all about the incredible powers Jesus had.

Story Stickers

These sticker pictures can be colored and cut out. Children can then use them for a wonderful variety of activities and crafts (see Introduction on page 3 for ideas).

The Wedding Feast at Cana—Page 6

The Miraculous Catch of Fish—Page 12

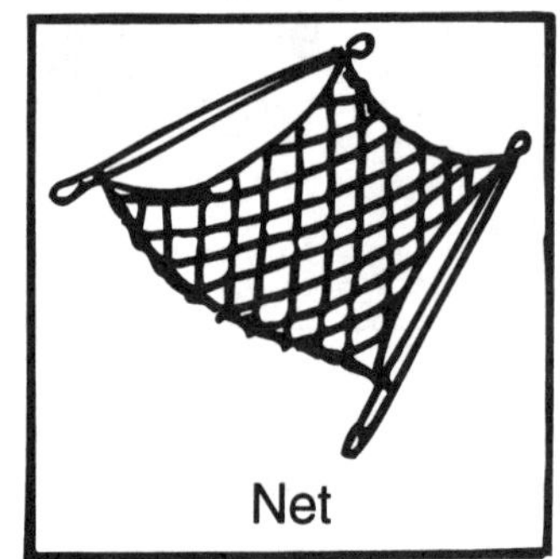

The Ten Lepers—Page 18

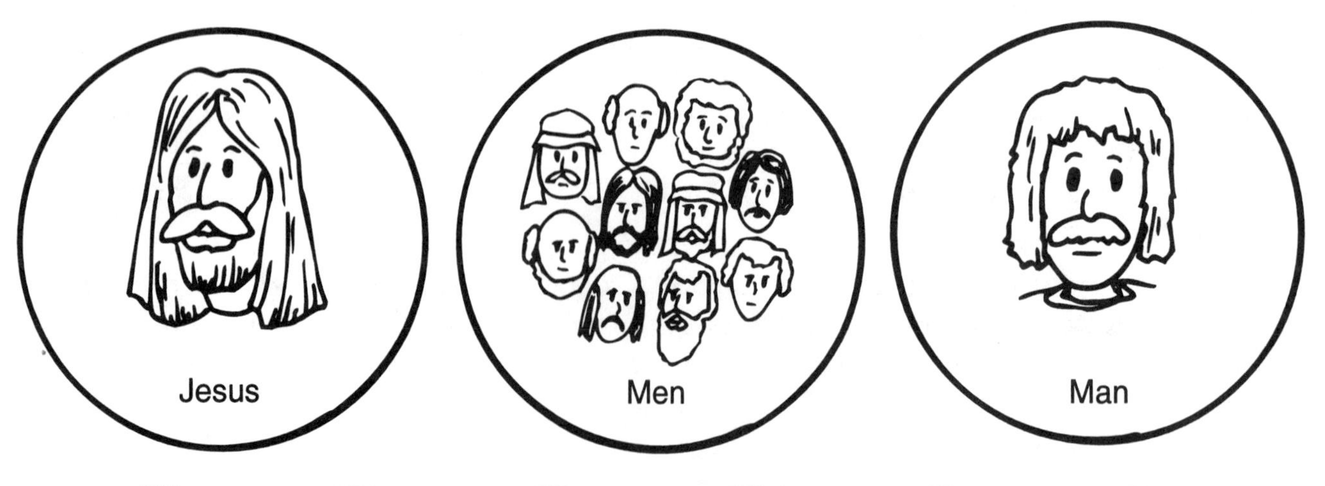

Story Stickers continued

The Loaves and Fish—Page 24

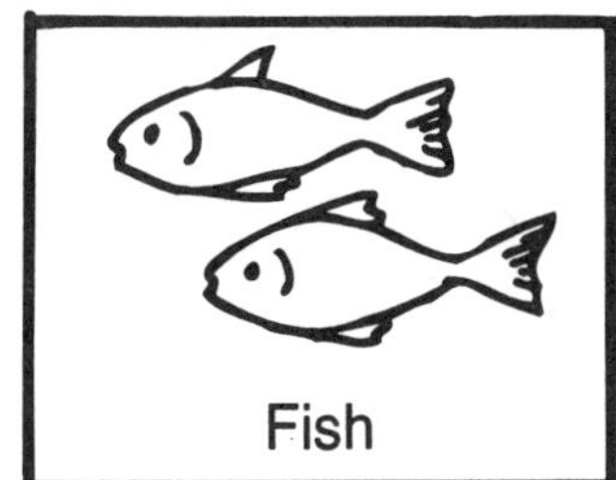

Jesus Cures a Paralyzed Man—Page 30

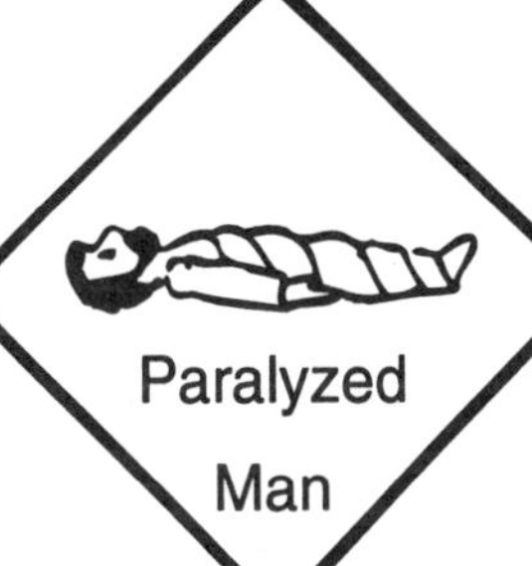

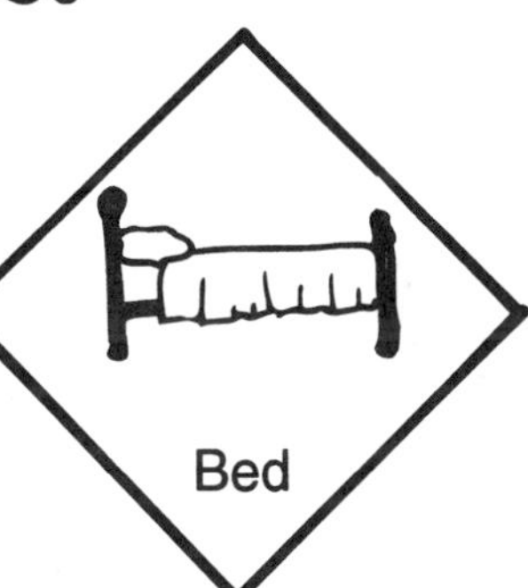

Jesus Calms a Storm—Page 36

Jesus Cures a Blind Beggar—Page 42

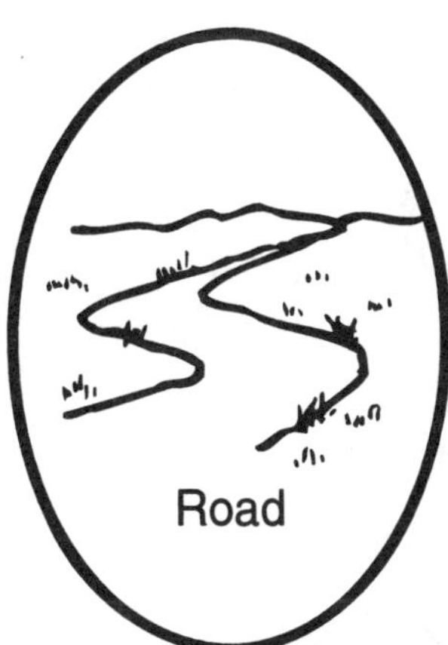

The Wedding Feast at Cana

(A Story Based on John 2:1–11)

Once,  was at a wedding feast.  , His mother, was there, too.  told  that there was no wine left.

 saw some large stone  .  told the  to fill the  with  . The  filled **1,2,3,4,5,6**  with  .

Then the  from the  was tasted.

Surprise! The  in the  had been changed into delicious wine. This was the first miracle performed.

A Wedding Celebration

. . . a wedding took place at Cana in Galilee . . . (John 2:1)

Circle 6 things that are wrong with this picture. Then color the picture.

All Gone

. . . *Jesus' mother said to him, "They have no more wine."* (John 2:3)

Count the empty wine goblets. Circle the number. Then color the picture.

1 2 3 4 5 6 7 8 9 10

Count the water jars. Circle the number. Then color the picture.

1 2 3 4 5 6 7 8 9 10

Fill Them Up!

Nearby stood six stone water jars . . . (John 2:6)

Color the matching jars the same color.

Finish the drawing. Make the second jar look the same as the first one.

Super Servers

Jesus said to the servants, "Fill the jars with water . . ." (John 2:7)

The lines show which servant filled each jar. Color each servant's clothing the same as the water jar he filled.

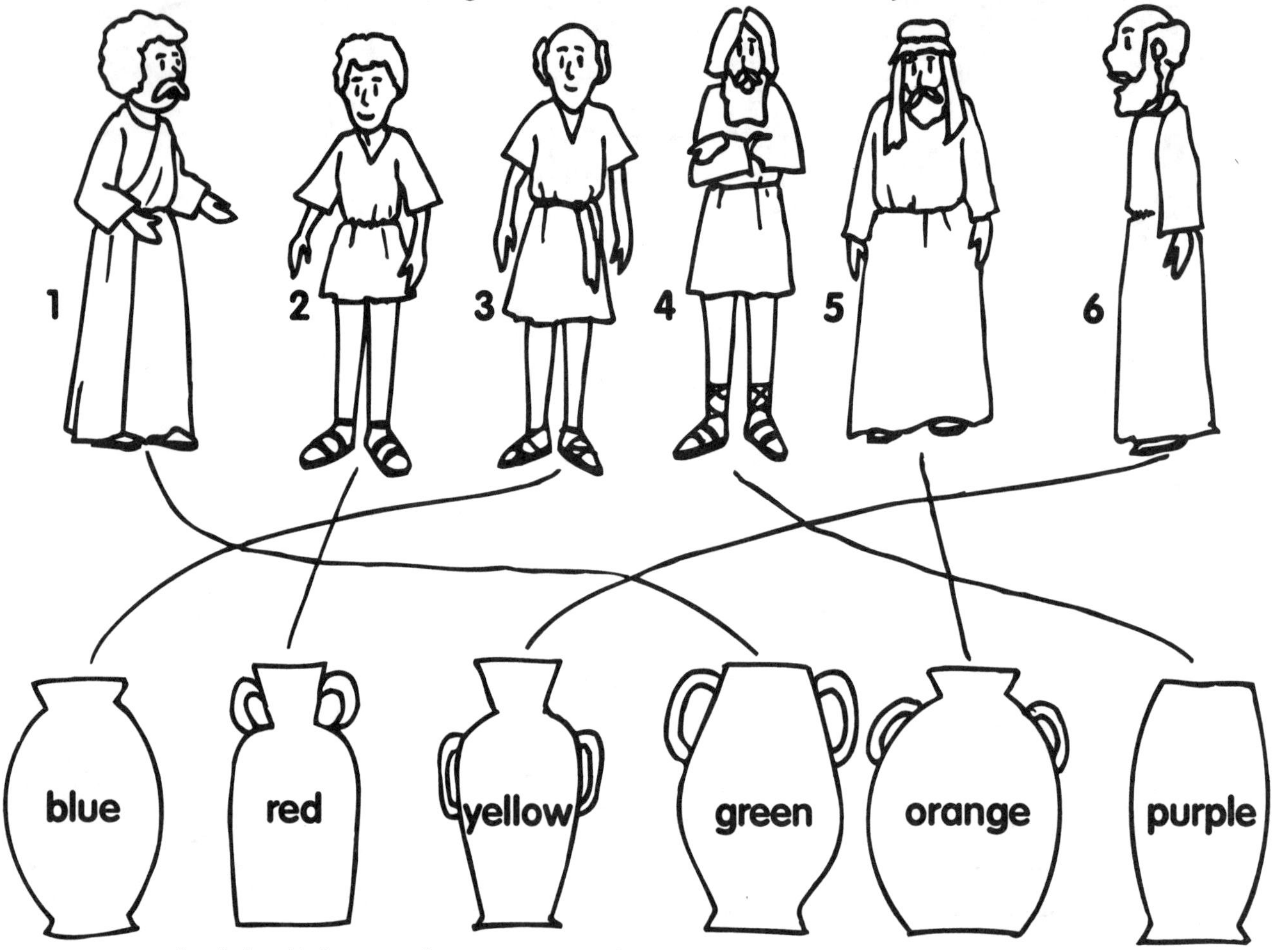

1 2 3 4 5 6

blue red yellow green orange purple

Inside this package are gifts to the bride and groom. Find and color the two hidden objects.

A Wedding Feast

(Sing to "Yankee Doodle.")

Once there was a wedding feast,
A wedding feast so fine.
Then Mary came to Jesus and said,
"Our hosts are out of wine."

Jesus saw six water jars
Standing in a line.
He had them filled with water.
Then He turned it into wine.

Water Jar (game)

Use six bowls, large milk cartons, or other containers to represent the six water jars in the story of the marriage feast at Cana. All six containers must be the same size. Set the water jars about ten feet away from a large bucket or tub of water. Choose six children to be servants. Give each servant a small plastic cup and assign each one a water jar to fill. The six servants dip their plastic cups into the large bucket or tub of water. Then each servant empties the water from the cup into his or her water jar. The children repeat this process over and over. When all the water jars are full, compliment the children by telling them they would have been good at helping on the day Jesus performed the miracle at Cana. Choose six different children for each of the next rounds.

Things to Discuss

Review how Jesus changed water into wine.

Discuss how the children have changed physically, mentally, and spiritually over the years. Can they ride a tricycle? How high can they count? How do they pray?

Discuss the changes the children would like to see made in the world.

Discuss how the world has changed since Jesus' time. Talk about clothing, houses, inventions, etc.

Discuss changes found in nature—leaves changing colors, caterpillars changing into butterflies, etc.

Things to Do

The first man to taste the wine Jesus made said it was better than the wine that had been served first. Conduct your own "wine tasting test." Serve two different grape juices or kinds of grapes. Have children close their eyes while you serve them each one. Which is the favorite?

The Miraculous Catch of Fish

(A Story Based on Luke 5:1–11)

One day,  got into a  to teach the  gathered near the . The  belonged to a fisherman named .

When  finished teaching, He told  to take the into deep  and to let down the . Soon, the  was full of . It began to break. The fishermen in another  came to help. Soon the   were full of . The fishermen were surprised. They had not been able to catch any  earlier.  told  that from then on, he would be catching men.

The fishermen gave up everything and followed .

Help! Help!

So they signaled their partners in the other boat to come and help them . . . (Luke 5:7)

Find and circle 7 differences in the bottom picture.

Net Trouble

. . . they caught such a large number of fish that their nets began to break. (Luke 5:6)

Color the picture according to the number code given.

1—red 2—yellow 3—green 4—blue

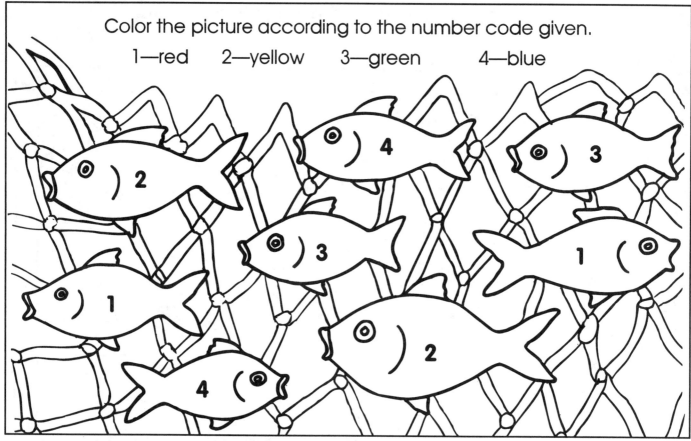

Count the fish in the net above. Then circle the correct number.

1 2 3 4 5 6 7 8 9 10

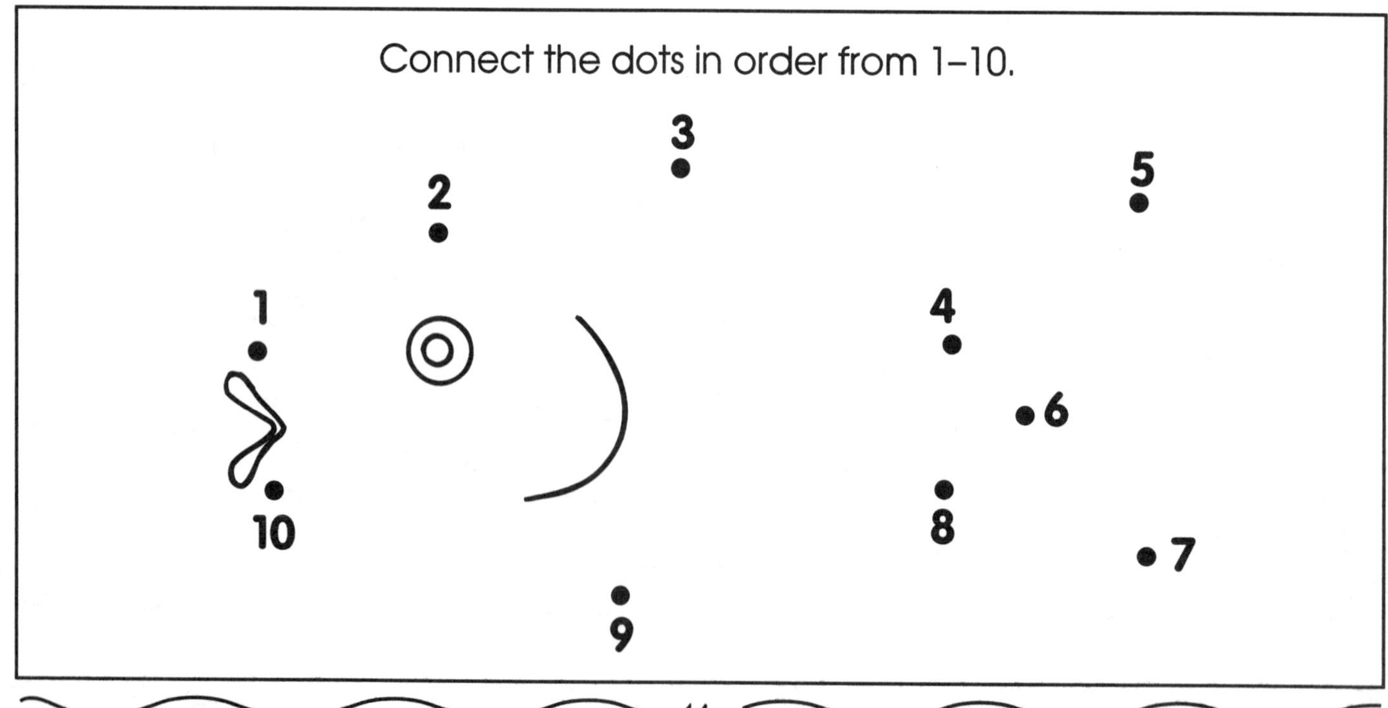

Connect the dots in order from 1–10.

So Many Fish!

For he and all his companions were astonished at the catch of fish they had taken.
(Luke 5:9)

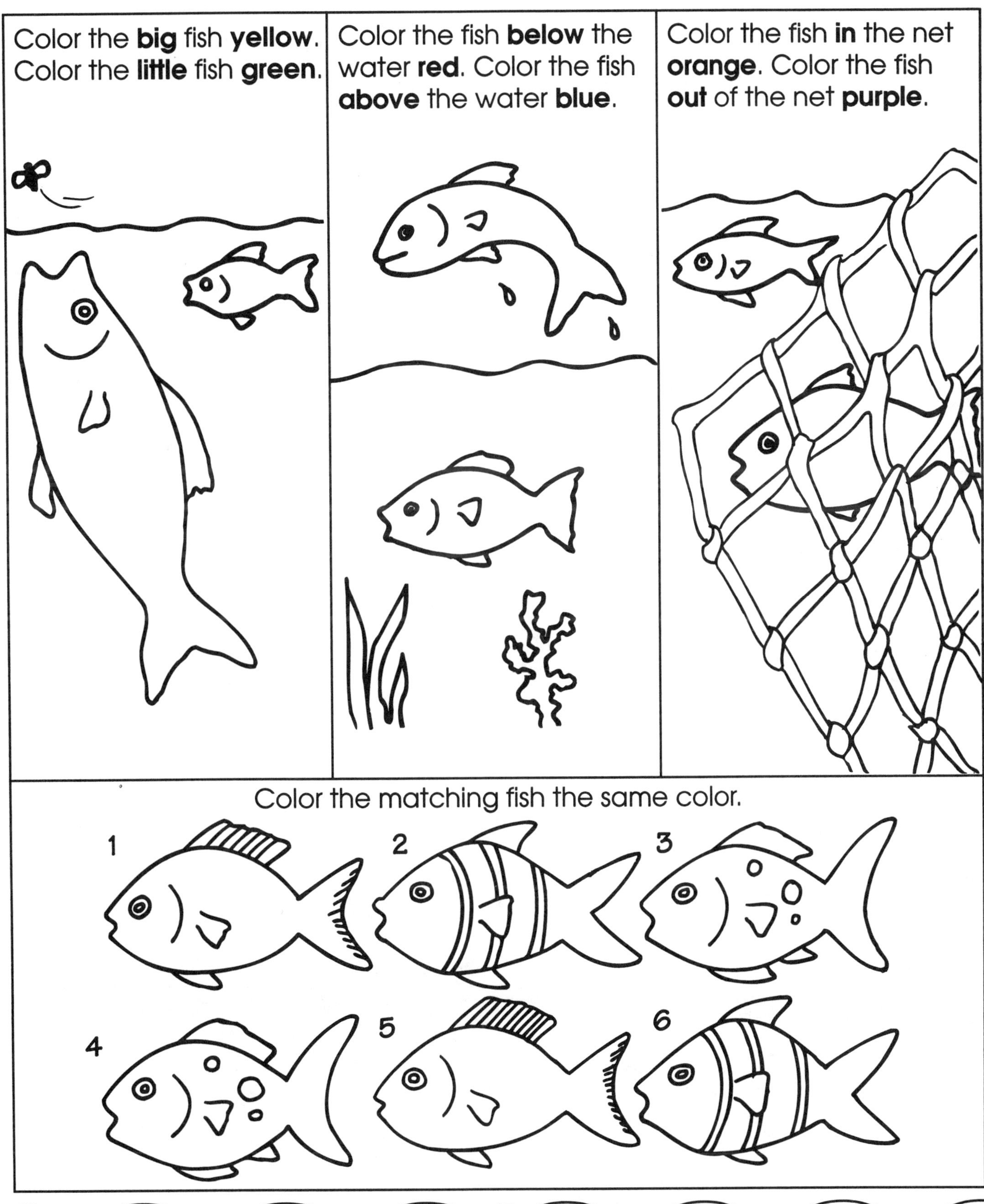

Color the **big** fish **yellow**. Color the **little** fish **green**.
Color the fish **below** the water **red**. Color the fish **above** the water **blue**.
Color the fish **in** the net **orange**. Color the fish **out** of the net **purple**.
Color the matching fish the same color.
1
2
3
4
5
6

See What We Caught!

. . . *"Put out into deep water, and let down the nets for a catch."* (Luke 5:4)

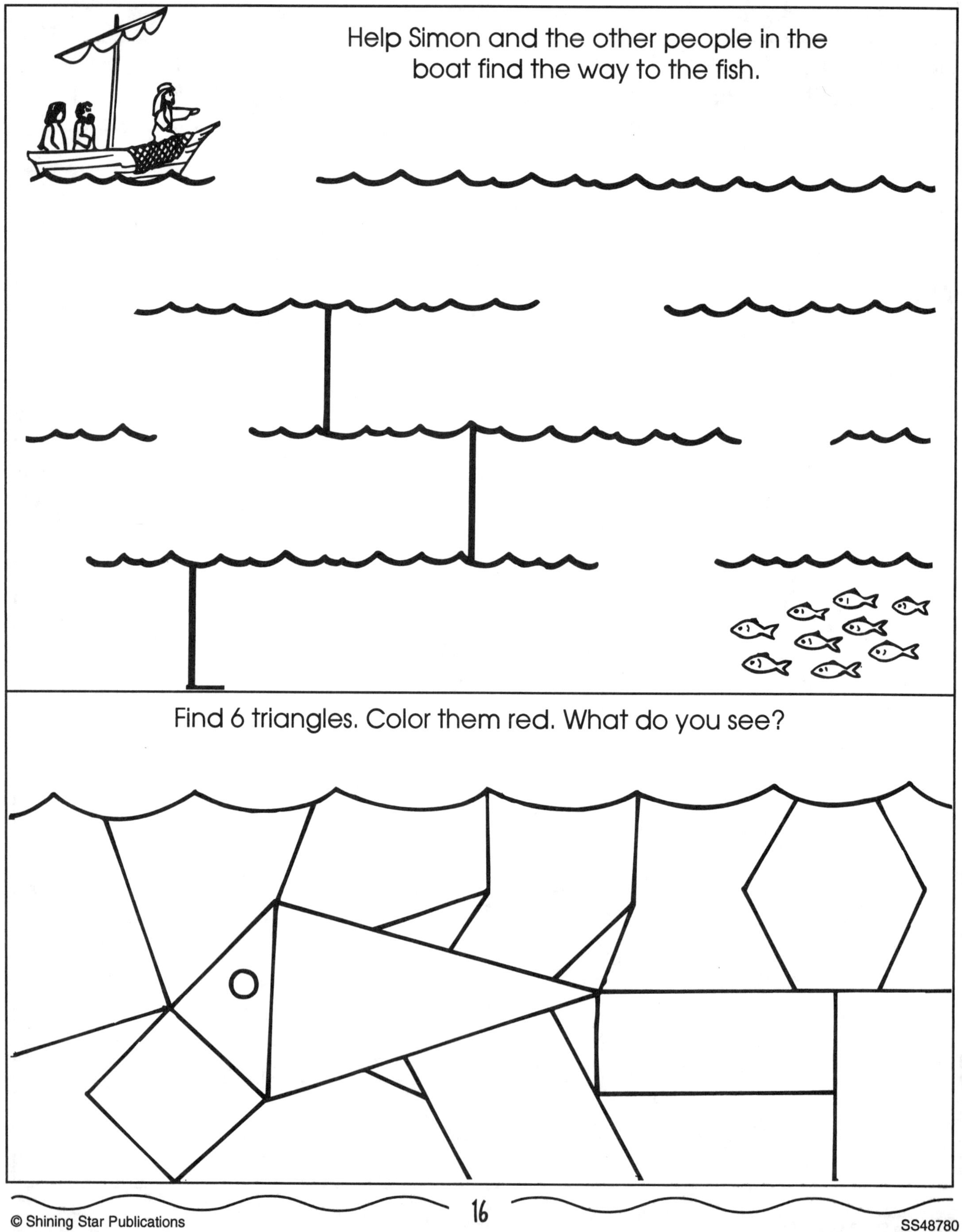

Help Simon and the other people in the boat find the way to the fish.
Find 6 triangles. Color them red. What do you see?

The Miraculous Catch

(Sing to "Row, Row, Row Your Boat.")

Crowds, crowds, crowds came up
To Jesus on the beach.
So Jesus got into a boat
And then began to teach.

"Row, row, row the boat,"
Jesus said when He was through.
So Simon rowed into the deep
As Jesus said to do.

"Cast, cast, cast your nets.
Try to catch some fish,"
Said Jesus to Simon,
Who did as Jesus wished.

Fish, fish filled the nets—
More than two boats could hold.
The catch of fish that had been caught
Was wondrous to behold!

Things to Do

Give each child a tagboard fish to decorate with sequins, macaroni, or whatever is available. Display them in a large net.

"Catch" children in the act of doing good and make it a point to praise them. Encourage them to catch each other doing good. Let children wear paper fish when they've been caught doing good.

Things to Discuss

Review how the fishermen gave up everything to follow Jesus.

Discuss how we follow Jesus when we do what is right. Present imaginary situations and ask the children what should be done in each case.

Go Fish (game)

Cut an equal number of fish and men out of tagboard. Attach a magnetic strip of tape to the back of each one. Put the fish and men, magnet side up, behind a tall box, a desk, or something through which the fishermen (children) can't see. Tie one end of a long piece of string to a magnet. Tie the other end to a pole (dowel rod, stick, yardstick, pointer, etc.). Let each child take a turn at being a fisherman. How many caught fish? How many were *fishers of men*? Tell all the children that they made a great catch.

The Ten Lepers

(A Story Based on Luke 17:11–19)

One day,  met **10** . The **10** 

had a skin disease. They cried out to  to heal them. 

told the **10**  to go and show themselves to the priests. On

the way, the **10**  were healed. **1** of them went back

to thank . **1,2,3,4,5,6,7,8,9** did not go back.

 was pleased with the  who returned.  told him that

his faith made him well.

Have Pity!

. . . They stood at a distance and called out in a loud voice, "Jesus, Master, have pity on us!" (Luke 17:12–13)

Find and color 10 things that have been added to the bottom picture.

Ten Sick Men

As he was going into a village, ten men who had leprosy met him . . . (Luke 17:12)

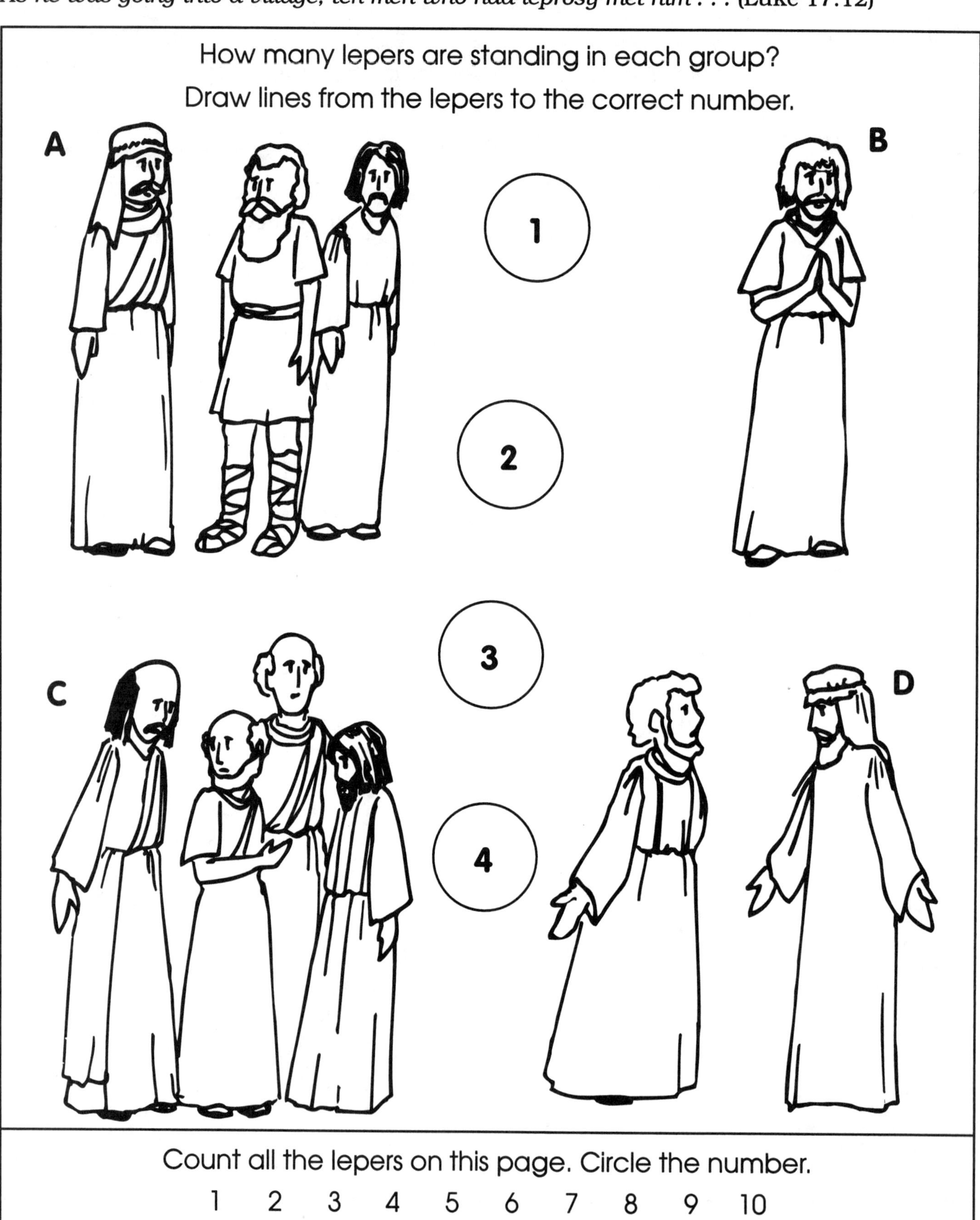

How many lepers are standing in each group?
Draw lines from the lepers to the correct number.
A
B
1
2
3
4
C
D
Count all the lepers on this page. Circle the number.
1 2 3 4 5 6 7 8 9 10

Nine Ungrateful Men

Jesus asked, "Were not all ten cleansed? Where are the other nine?" (Luke 17:17)

Below are the 9 lepers who did not return to thank Jesus.

Draw an **X** on the leper who is **sitting**.

1

2

3

Draw a **line** under the **tallest** leper.

4

5

6

Draw a **circle** around the **oldest** leper.

7

8

9

One Thankful Man

One of them, when he saw he was healed, came back, praising God in a loud voice. He threw himself at Jesus' feet and thanked him—and he was a Samaritan. (Luke 17:15–16)

Which leper returned to thank Jesus? Follow each path to find out. Then draw a heart on the thankful leper.

Jesus Cures Ten Lepers

(Sing to "Ten Little Indians.")

1 little, 2 little, 3 little lepers,
4 little, 5 little, 6 little lepers,
7 little, 8 little, 9 little lepers . . .
10 lepers cured one day.

Lepers 1, 2, and 3 went on their ways.
Lepers 4, 5, and 6 went on their ways.
Lepers 7, 8, and 9 went on their ways . . .
But leper 10 returned in praise.

Things to Do

Have children design thank-you cards showing things others have done for them.

Let each child make a "Word of Thanks" project. For each child, cut out the word THANKS from a large sheet of brightly colored construction paper. The letters should all be connected, and they should be as large as possible. Let children cover the word with drawings or magazine pictures of the things for which they are thankful. An option is to write THANKS on a large sheet of butcher paper and let all the children draw pictures on it to form a large mural.

Follow the Cured Leper (game)

The lepers must have been excited to have their body parts free of the skin disease. Let children experience this joy. Let each child take a turn being the *cured leper* leader. Other children follow the joyous actions (skipping, jumping, etc.) of the leader. Children might like putting their movements to music.

Things to Discuss

Review how only one of the cured lepers came back to praise God and thank Jesus.

Discuss the importance of not taking things for granted. Then have a spontaneous "Thank You, God, for . . ." prayer time in which children mention things for which they are thankful.

Thank You, God!

The Loaves and Fish

(A Story Based on John 6:1–13)

One day, many  came to listen to . The people were hungry. One  had **5** loaves of  and **2** small , but how could so little food feed  thousand hungry ?

 told His disciples to make the  sit down. Then  gave thanks for the  and . The disciples gave the  and  to the . The  ate as much food as they wanted. Then  told His disciples to gather what was left. The leftovers filled **12** !

Not a Lot of Food

"'Here is a boy with five small barley loaves and two small fish, but how far will they go among so many?'" (John 6:9)

Hidden in the picture are 5 loaves of bread and 2 fish. Find and color them.

A Lot of Leftovers

. . . they . . . filled twelve baskets with the pieces of the five barley loaves left over by those who had eaten. (John 6:13)

Trace the numbers from 1–12.

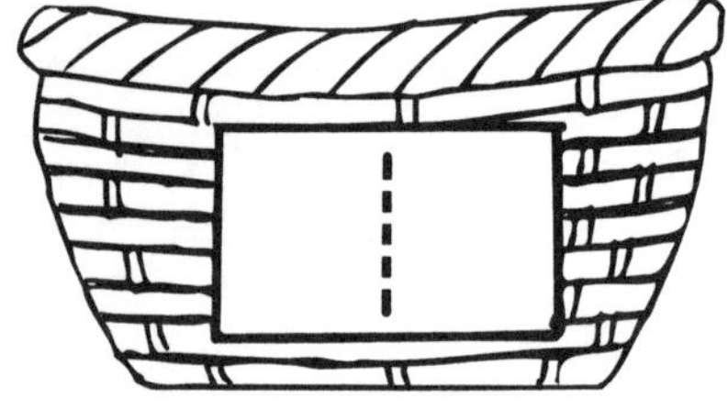

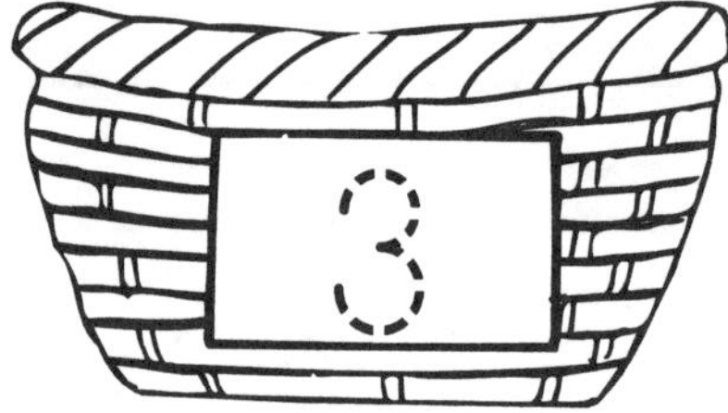

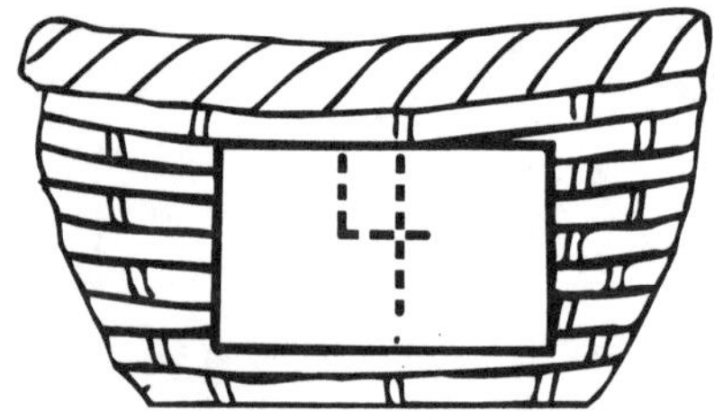

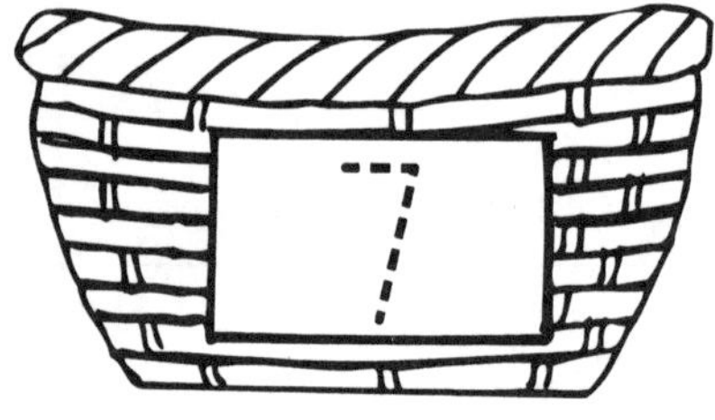

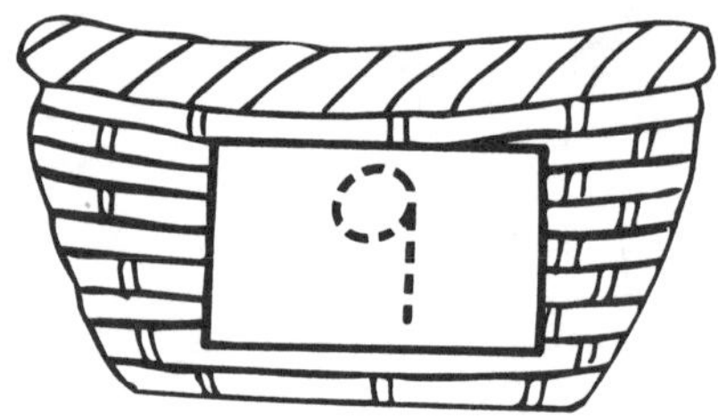

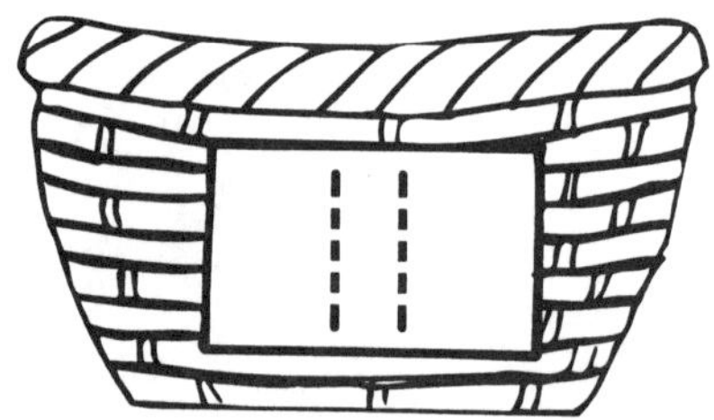

Optional—Listen to and follow the directions.

Draw a circle around Basket 8.
Draw a loaf of bread in Basket 7.
Use blue to color Basket 3.
Draw a line under Basket 2.
Draw one fish in Basket 4.
Use red to color Basket 1.

Draw an X on Basket 11.
Draw a box around Basket 10.
Use green to color Basket 12.
Use brown to color Basket 9.
Use yellow to color Basket 5.
Draw two fish in Basket 6.

Sit and Eat

Jesus said, "Have the people sit down" . . . (John 6:10)

Circle the people who are sitting.

Use an **X** to cross out the one in each row that is not the same.

Do Not Waste!

. . . he said to his disciples, "Gather the pieces that are left over. Let nothing be wasted." (John 6:12)

Complete the pattern. Draw what comes next in each row.

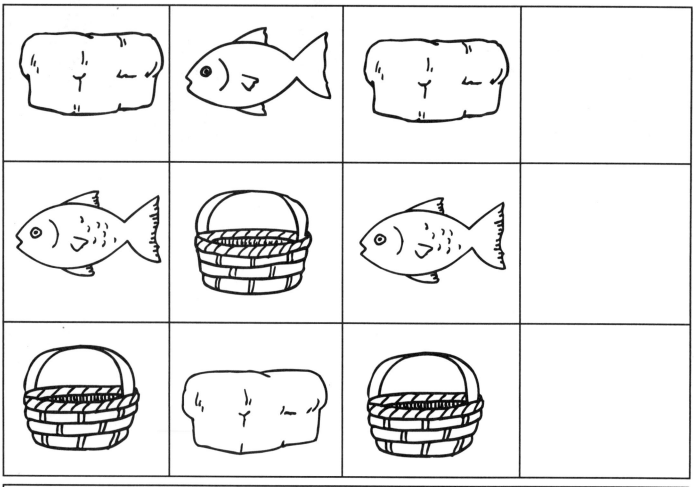

Two fish are hidden in this puzzle. Find and color them.
Be careful! Some are just leftover pieces of fish.

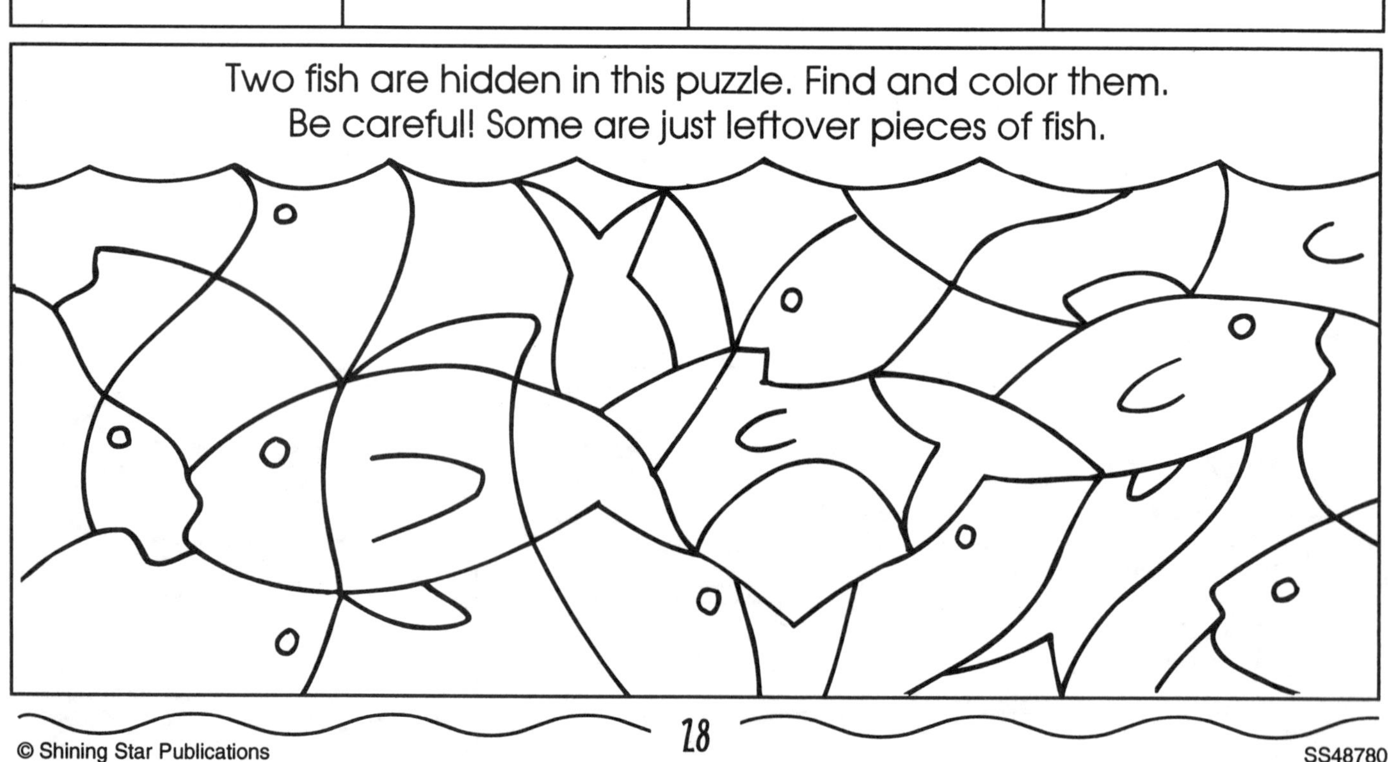

Song, Game, and Idea Page

The Loaves and Fish

(Sing to "London Bridge.")

A boy once had five barley loaves,
Barley loaves, barley loaves.
A boy once had five barley loaves
And two small fish.

Jesus blessed the loaves and fish,
Loaves and fish, loaves and fish.
Jesus blessed the loaves and fish
And fed five thousand.

The disciples gathered what remained,
What remained, what remained.
The disciples gathered what remained
And filled twelve baskets.

Things to Do

Jesus told the disciples to gather up what remained of the loaves and fish so that nothing would be wasted. Gather up scraps of material, old buttons, lids, empty cartons, etc. Let children create an art project from all the scraps.

Jesus fed the hungry with just a few loaves of bread and fish. Have each child bring in just a few food items to help feed a hungry family in the community.

Let children multiply their vocabularies by having them learn the names of the different kinds of breads below.

barley	rye
wheat	white
sourdough	pumpernickel
corn bread	English muffin

Things to Discuss

Review how Jesus made just a little amount of food go a long way.

Discuss how a little smile, greeting card, help, or prayer can go a long way.

Discuss recycling.

Ask children to think of as many uses as they can for an empty egg carton.

Loaf Toss (game)

Crumple five pieces of scrap paper to serve as scraps of bread left over after the miracle Jesus performed. Let each child take a turn tossing the scraps into a basket (or box decorated as a basket) set about six feet away. Vary the distance depending on the children's ages. Can anyone toss all five scraps into the basket? If time permits, let each child toss again and again until all five scraps are inside the basket.

Jesus Cures a Paralyzed Man

(A Story Based on Mark 2:1–12)

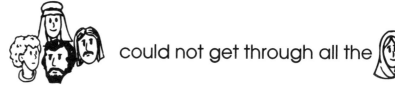

One day, many  crowded inside a 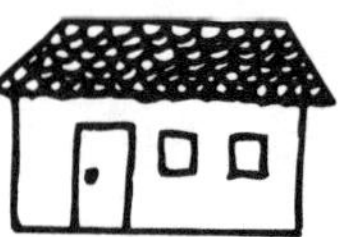 and outside the  to hear . 4  tried to carry a  to . The 4  could not get through all the .

They climbed on the  and made a  in it. Then they lowered the  on his  down through the .  forgave the 's sins. He told the  who couldn't walk to pick up his  and go home. The  did, and everyone was amazed.

Good Friends

Since they could not get him to Jesus because of the crowd, they made an opening in the roof above Jesus and, after digging through it, lowered the mat the paralyzed man was lying on. (Mark 2:4)

The man who couldn't walk had 4 friends with loving hearts. Find 4 hearts hidden in the picture. Color them red. Then color the rest of the picture.

Home Sweet Home

. . . the people heard that he had come home. (Mark 2:1)

Circle the answer to each question.

How many roof tiles? Count each triangle.	1	2	3	4	5	6	7	8	9	10
How many windows? Count each square.	1	2	3	4	5	6	7	8	9	10
How many doors? Count each rectangle.	1	2	3	4	5	6	7	8	9	10
How many stones? Count each circle.	1	2	3	4	5	6	7	8	9	10

Hearts of Love

Immediately Jesus knew in his spirit that this was what they were thinking in their hearts, and he said to them, "Why are you thinking these things?" (Mark 2:8)

Color the **little** heart **blue**.
Color the **big** heart **red**.

Color the heart on the **top purple**.
Color the heart on the **bottom green**.

Color the heart on the **right orange**.
Color the heart on the **left yellow**.

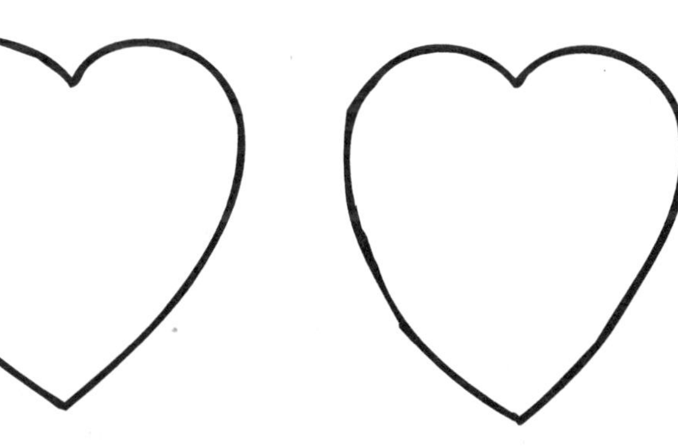

Color the **fancy** heart **purple**.
Color the **plain** heart **orange**.

Color the one with **many** hearts **red**.
Color the one with **few** hearts **green**.

Color the one with the **happy** face **yellow**.
Color the one with the **sad** face **blue**.

What Good Friends!

Some men came, bringing to him a paralytic, carried by four of them. (Mark 2:3)

Draw a line from each friend to his matching shadow.

Jesus Cures a Paralyzed Man

(Sing to "Mary Had a Little Lamb.")

There was a man who couldn't walk,
Couldn't walk, couldn't walk.
There was a man who couldn't walk,
So he laid upon a bed.

He was carried by four friends one day,
Friends one day, friends one day.
He was carried by four friends one day
To a house where Jesus preached.

There was a large crowd in the way,
In the way, in the way.
There was a large crowd in the way,
So they climbed upon a roof.

They lowered the man through the roof,
Through the roof, through the roof.
They lowered the man through the roof
To Jesus down below.

Jesus said, "Get up and walk,
Up and walk, up and walk."
Jesus said, "Get up and walk,"
And at once, the man was cured.

Things to Do

Have children make cards or favors or have them color pictures for shut-ins, hospital patients, or friends confined to bed.

Have one group of children lie very still for five or ten minutes while the other children dance and play. Then let the children exchange places. Discuss how it felt to be paralyzed.

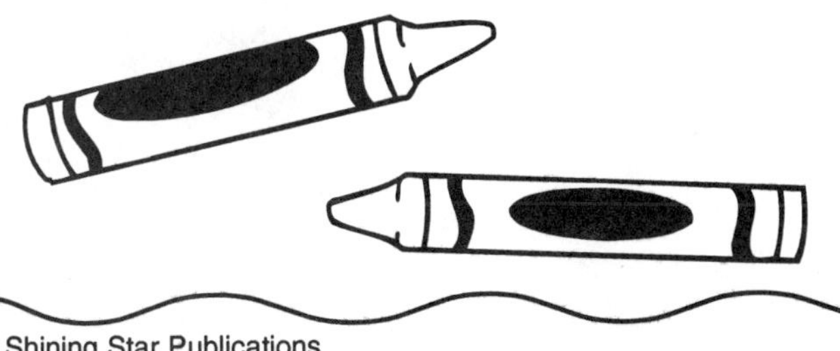

The Roof (game)

Divide children into lines of four to represent the four friends who brought the paralyzed man to Jesus. For each group of four, you will need to lay four blocks (wooden, plastic, or paper) on the ground about ten feet away from a starting line. The object of the game is to open the roof by removing all four blocks. To start the game, the first child on each team runs, picks up a block, and brings it back across the starting line. Then the next players take turns until the team has removed all four blocks and brought them across the starting line. When each team finishes, tell the children on that team that they are good friends. Very young children may not have been involved in a relay before. It would be very helpful for an adult or older child to be in charge of each group to guide the children along during the relay.

Things to Discuss

Discuss the faith and determination of the friends who brought the paralyzed man to Jesus.

Discuss the importance of being a good friend others can count on. Discuss ways of being a good friend.

Jesus Calms a Storm

(A Story Based on Mark 4:35–41)

One day,  was sleeping on a  when it began to storm. A strong  began to blow.  crashed into the . The  became full of . The  on the  were afraid. They woke  up.  told the  and the  to be still. The  and the became calm.

The  on the  were a little frightened by this miracle. They were amazed that the  and the  obeyed !

Be Still!

He got up, rebuked the wind and said to the waves, "Quiet! Be still!" Then the wind died down and it was completely calm. (Mark 4:39)

After Jesus calmed the storm, many things changed.
Circle 6 things in the bottom picture that are not the same in the top picture.

Story Fun

Number the pictures from 1–4 in the order they happened in the Bible story.

He got up . . . (Mark 4:39)

Jesus was . . . sleeping . . . (Mark 4:38)

. . . The disciples woke him . . . (Mark 4:38)

. . . Then the wind died down and it was completely calm. (Mark 4:39)

Wavy Water

. . . and the waves broke over the boat . . . (Mark 4:37)

Color the 2 in each row that are alike.

What a Storm!

A furious squall came up . . . (Mark 4:37)

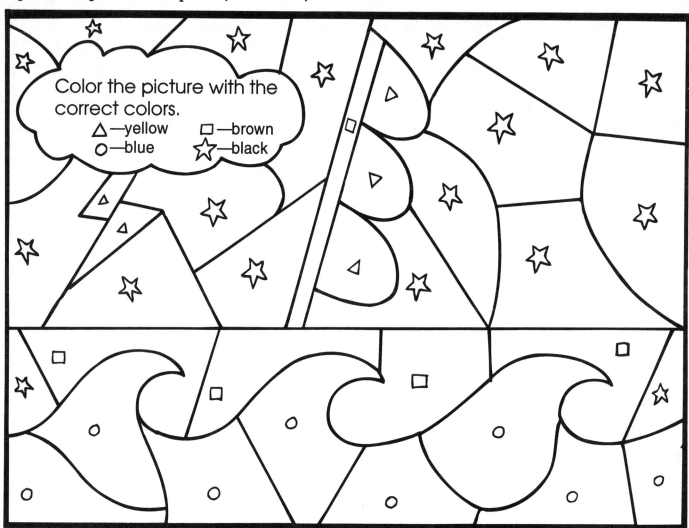

Color the picture with the correct colors.

△—yellow □—brown

○—blue ☆—black

Draw 2 more.

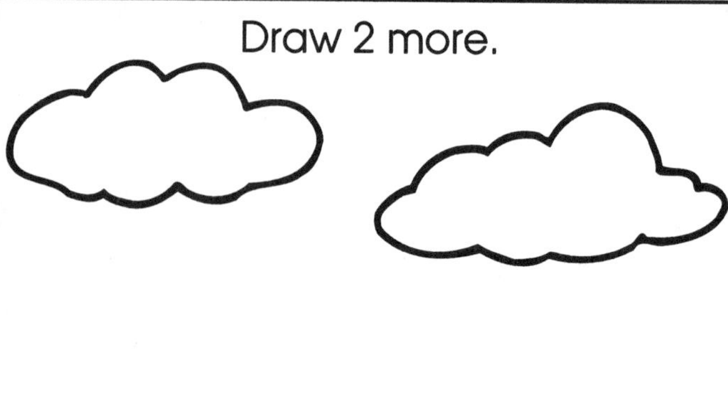

How many in all? Circle the number.

1 2 3 4 5 6 7 8 9 10

Draw 4 more.

How many in all? Circle the number.

1 2 3 4 5 6 7 8 9 10

Jesus Calms a Storm

(Sing to "Are You Sleeping?")

Jesus was sleeping.
Jesus was sleeping.
The wind began to blow.
The wind began to blow.
The waves grew higher and higher.
The waves grew higher and higher.
The boat tossed to and fro.
The boat tossed to and fro.

"Why are you sleeping?
Why are you sleeping?"
The disciples asked in fear.
The disciples asked in fear.
"The boat is almost sinking.
The boat is almost sinking.
The end is surely near.
The end is surely near."

Then Jesus calmed the wind.
Then Jesus calmed the wind.
And Jesus calmed the waves.
And Jesus calmed the waves.
The wind and waves obeyed Him.
The wind and waves obeyed Him.
The disciples were amazed.
The disciples were amazed.

Things to Discuss

Review the story and discuss how the disciples were afraid of the storm even though they knew Jesus was with them.

Discuss children's fears and ways to handle those fears. Talk about how God is always with us and how prayer can help to calm fears.

Windstorm (game)

Each child will need a sheet of paper that has been crumpled into a ball. The crumpled paper represents the boat in the Bible story. Mark off a start and finish line with chalk, yarn, or masking tape. The lines should be parallel to each other, about 20 feet apart. The area between the two lines is the lake. The object of the game is to blow the boat across the lake. Let children race in groups of 5 or 6. Each child places his or her boat on the starting line. Then each lines up on hands and knees behind the boat. Pronounce each child a winner when he or she gets the boat across the finish line. Children must rely only on their own "windstorm" to move the boat. They may not touch the boat with any parts of their bodies.

Things to Do

Let children toss together a treat in a boat. Let each start with a boat-shaped container, such as those commonly used for banana splits. Let them toss in some scoops of ice cream. Have them add two banana "half oars." Next, a lake of syrup can be splashed on top. A whipped cream fog can form the next layer. Finally, they can add a downpour of candy sprinkles or chopped nuts. Children will love their storm-tossed dessert boats.

Jesus Cures a Blind Beggar

(A Story Based on Mark 10:46–52)

One day, a  sat by the side of the  begging.

Someone told the  that  was walking by. The 

cried out to . Some  told the  to be quiet.

Instead, the  cried out again.  stopped. The 

stood up and went forward when he was called.  asked the 

what he wanted. The  wanted to see.  told the 

his faith had healed him. Suddenly, the  was able to see!

A Poor Blind Man

. . . a blind man, Bartimaeus . . . was sitting by the roadside begging. (Mark 10:46)

The blind beggar would not have been able to see the 8 animals hidden in this picture. Can you? Find and color them.

What a Sight!

. . . Immediately he received his sight and followed Jesus along the road. (Mark 10:52)

After he was cured, the blind man followed Jesus. Can you follow the dots? Connect the dots from 1–10 to find something the man could now see.

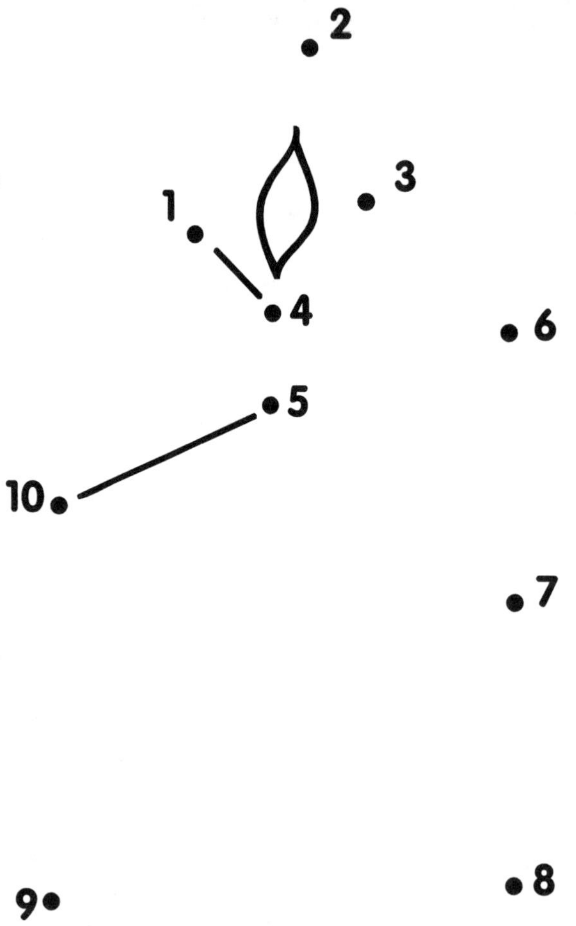

Color the picture the correct colors. 1—yellow 2—blue

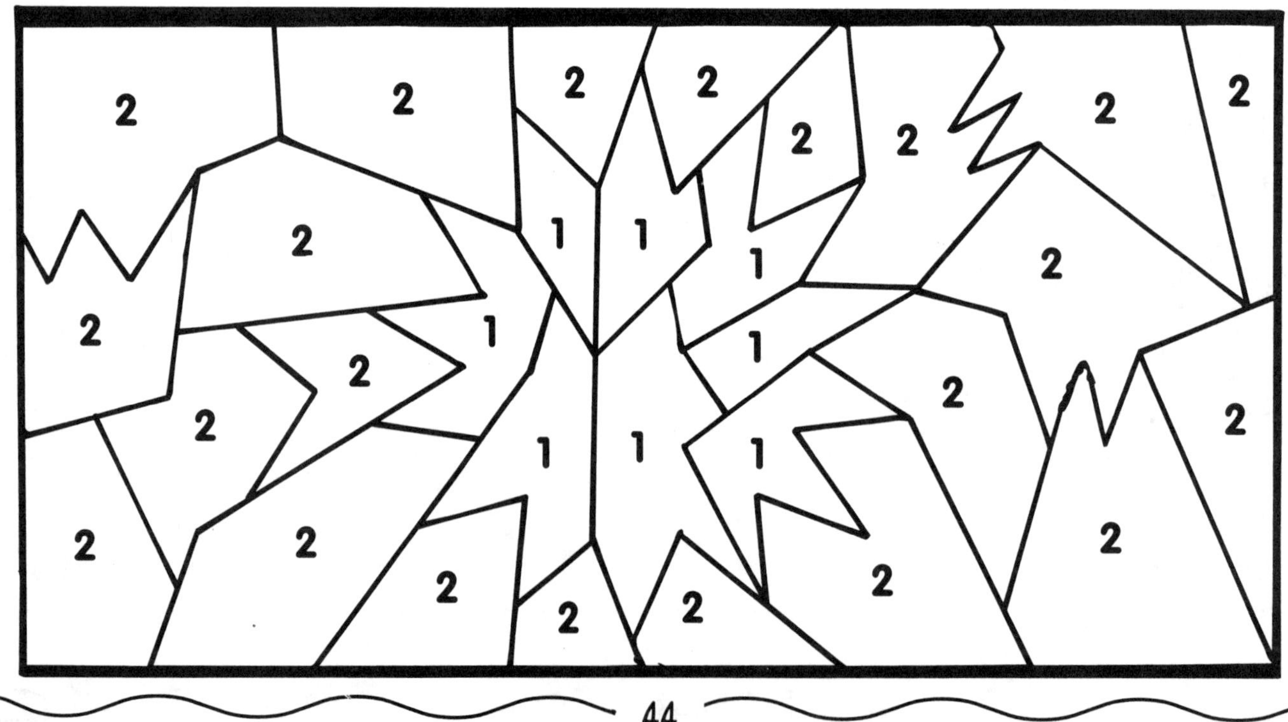

SS48780

Look at This!

. . . The blind man said, "Rabbi, I want to see." (Mark 10:51)

Color the matching eyes the same color.

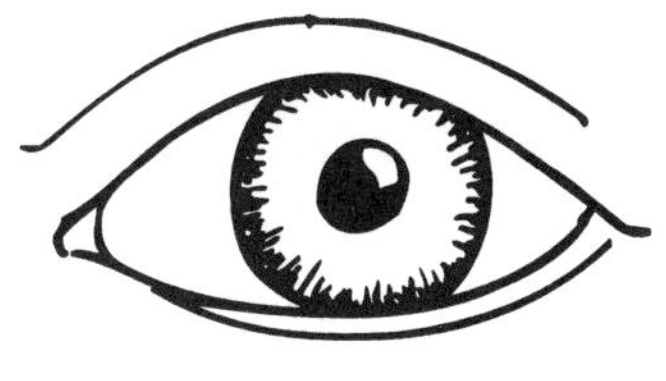

1

2

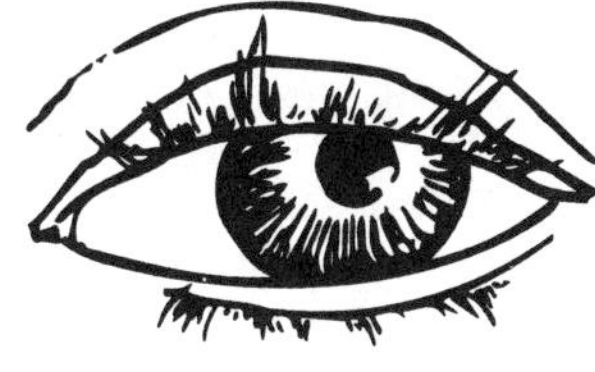

3

4

5

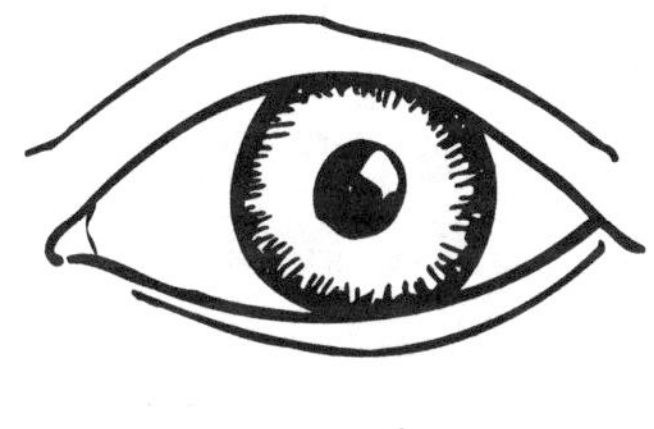

6

Look closely at each person's eyes.
Circle the one who is sleepy.
Underline the one who is sad.
Put an **X** on the one who is surprised.

Here I Am!

Throwing his cloak aside, he jumped to his feet and came to Jesus. (Mark 10:50)

Help the blind man make his way safely to Jesus.

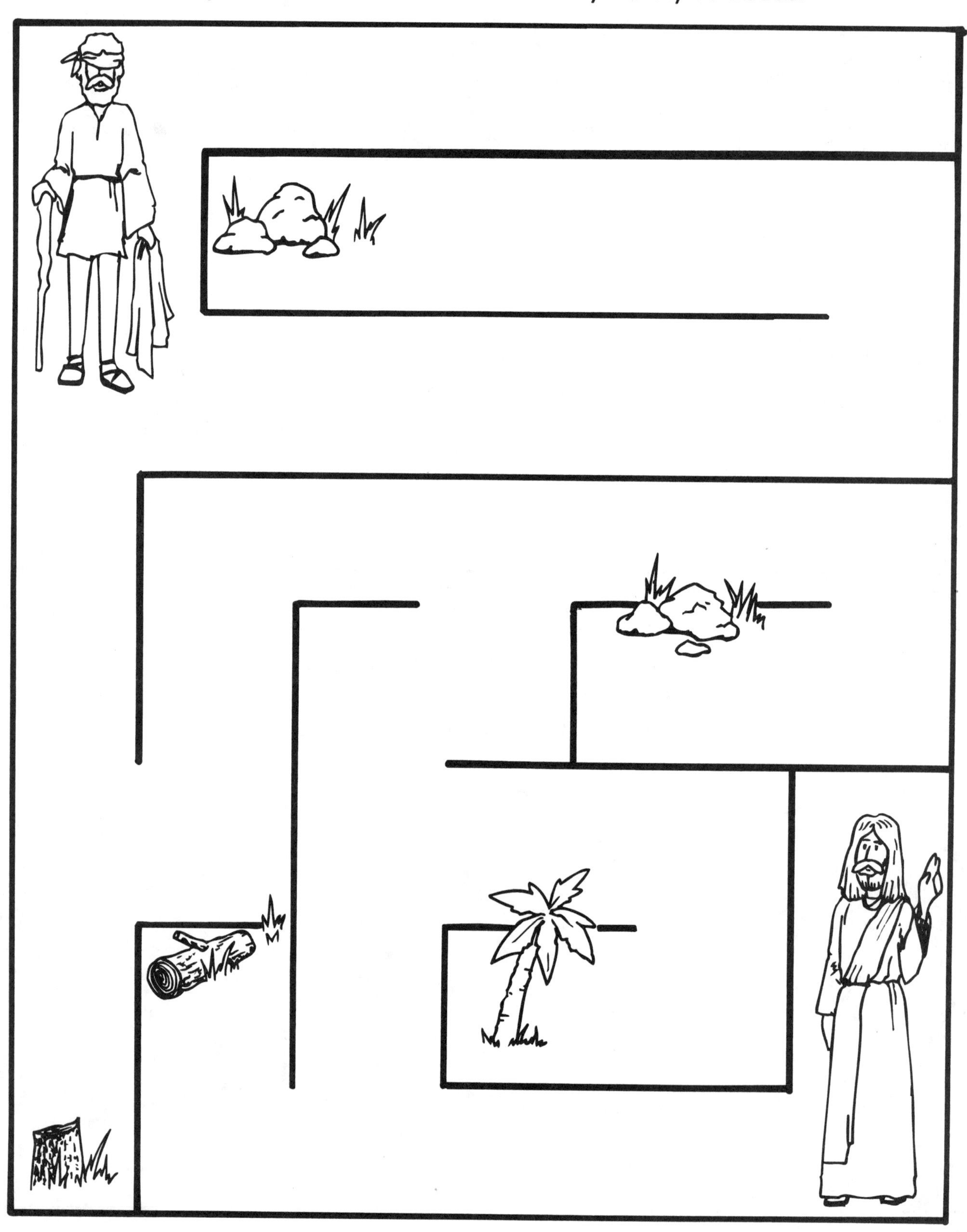

SS48780

Jesus Cures a Blind Man

(Sing to "Three Blind Mice.")

One blind beggar, one blind beggar,
Cried out to Jesus. Cried out to Jesus.
"Son of David, have mercy on me.
Cure my blindness, I beg of thee."
"Because of your faith, you now can see,"
Jesus told the beggar. Jesus told the beggar.

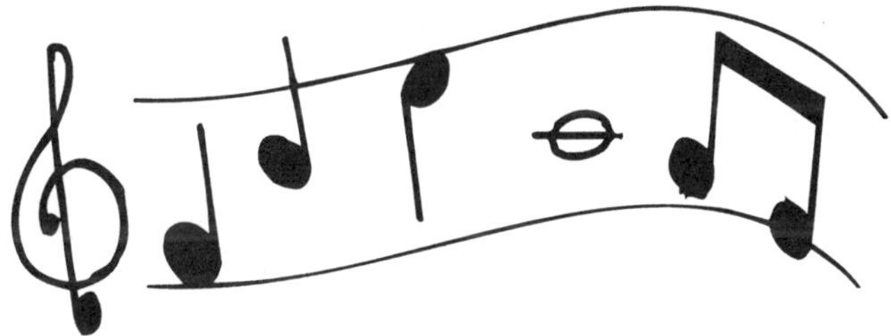

Things to Do

Let the children look at things such as insects and pond water under a microscope or magnifying glass. They will discover a new way of seeing things.

Take an awareness walk and ask children to point out things they never really noticed before but may have passed every day.

Bring in photos of parts of objects or objects taken at unusual angles. Ask children to guess the identities of the objects.

Let children decorate paper candles to symbolize Jesus as the light of the world.

Things to Discuss

Review the story of the blind man and how Jesus cured him because of his faith.

Discuss things children enjoy seeing most (cartoons, butterflies, etc.) and ask them to imagine what it would be like if they couldn't see those things.

Discuss how we are sometimes blind to the needs of others (ignoring a child who has no one to play with, pretending not to see someone who needs our help, etc.).

Discuss how we are sometimes blind to what God wants us to do.

Guess What It Is (game)

Children's eyes should be shut or blindfolded for this game. They will need to rely on senses other than sight to identify objects. For round one, put an object in a bag. Let each child touch it. Then ask the children to guess what the object is. For round two, let children listen to a sound and then ask them to identify the object that made the sound. For round three, place something to taste in each child's mouth. Ask children to identify the food. For the final round, let each child smell an open container of something. Then ask the children to guess what is making the scent.

Answer Key

Page 7

Page 8
5, 6

Page 9
1 and 5, 2 and 6, 3 and 4

Page 10
1—green, 2—red, 3—blue, 4—purple, 5—orange, 6—yellow; gifts: 2 goblets

Page 13

Page 14
8 fish

Page 15
1 and 5, 2 and 6, 3 and 4

Page 16
a fish

Page 19

Page 20
1—B, 2—D, 3—A, 4—C; 10

Page 21
2, 6, 7

Page 22
leper 8

Page 25

Page 27
1, 2, 4; 3rd loaf, 2nd fish, 1st basket

Page 28
fish, basket, loaf of bread

Page 31

Page 32
9, 3, 1, 8

Page 34
1—D, 2—B, 3—A, 4—C

Page 37

Page 38
Top—3, 1; Bottom—2, 4

Page 39
1st and 3rd waves, 1st and 2nd boats, 2nd and 3rd clouds, 1st and 3rd pictures

Page 40
4, 7

Page 43

Page 44
candle, sun in the sky

Page 45
1 and 6, 2 and 4, 3 and 5; underline, X, circle